Hello!
Heaven Is Speaking, *Are You Listening?*

Wanda Pollydore

authorHOUSE®

AuthorHouse™
1663 Liberty Drive
Bloomington, IN 47403
www.authorhouse.com
Phone: 1 (800) 839-8640

First Publication at AuthorHouse on 1/24/2011

Revised by AuthorHouse 12/26/2017

ISBN: 978-1-4520-9067-2 (sc)
ISBN: 978-1-4520-9066-5 (hc)
ISBN: 978-1-4520-9068-9 (e)

Library of Congress Control Number: 2010916437

Print information available on the last page.

This book is printed on acid-free paper.

Contents

The Truth Shall Make You Free

John: 8:32 (KJV) "And ye shall know the truth, and the truth shall make you free."
John: 8:32 (AMP) "And you will know the Truth, and the Truth will set you free."

Parallel scriptures:
John: 14:6 (KJV) "Jesus saith unto him, I am the way, the truth, and the life: no man cometh unto the Father, but by me."
John: 14:6 (AMP) "Jesus said to him, I am the way and the truth and the life; no one comes to the Father except by (through) me."
Matthew: 4:4 (KJV) "But he answered and said, It is written, man shall not live by bread alone, but by every word that proceedeth out of the mouth of God."

Matthew: 4:4 (AMP) "But he replied, it has been written, man shall not live and be upheld and sustained by bread alone, but by every word that comes forth from the mouth of God."

The Merriam Webster Dictionary: defines Truth as confirmation to fact or actuality; reality; actual statement proven to be or accepted as true. It also defines sincerity as "integrity, truth" and defines Christian science as "God."

The Truth Shall Make You Free:

The unshakableness of God is Christ. The unshakable truth of God was made flesh and came directly to man by the will of God. The image of God is infinite and seen in all of humanity, whether attractive or unattractive according to the human eye.

Matthew: 24:14 (KJV) "And this gospel of the Kingdom shall be preached in all the world for a witness unto all nations; and then shall the end come." Christ said to the multitude, "My Ways are Higher." It was distinguishing that His ways were better than the worlds. It is one thing to stray away from the truth, but don't stay away; it can be dangerous.

God gave everyone a soul People usually live life the way they see it. You will be judged for your deed(s), not someone else's. This is the actual fairness of truth, thank God! However, we are punished from time to time for our deed(s). Although were under the grace of God, the punishment is the result of not listening to him.

God is not punishing us, we are punishing ourselves because He will not lie, trick, or rob us. Only Love, Light, and Truth exist in God. God can use negative situations for good. We can look through the Bible and see God used the children of Israel's enemies to bless them. God can do the same for us today. The truth is the two most powerful things in this world are sex and money—not necessarily in that order. One is use to get the other or vice versa. There are so many people who fear the truth. God loves people who are inquisitive about him and do not fear. People will be fed according to their spiritual level. It is not wise to go beyond your level, because your mind will become like a flour sifter and the information will disappear.

John: 14:1 (KJV) "Let not your heart be troubled: ye believe in God, believe also in me."

Christ's physical body was the veil torn from top to bottom. This society has made others pay a heavy price for the truth, such as imprisonment or even death. It is unfortunate that this society allows deceitfulness to be acceptable. There are four professions—doctors, lawyers, politicians, and pastors, that all have two things in common: each of them take an oath to up hold their position and the other is that they withhold the truth. Doctors know which medicines can cure people, but disclosing the information will put the majority of them out of business. Lawyers have client(s) who have disclosed to them their guilt but remain loyal to their clients claiming "attorney-client privilege."

Politicians make all kinds of promises while campaigning. They know where the money is to correct the deficit in order to get the economy out of a crisis but what do they do? They take some for themselves and hide the rest. Pastors know the true gospel but will not reveal its truth; it is not for the masses. These individuals do not want to interfere with the status quo. It does not matter who you are or who you say you are, your decisions and past will catch up with you. We must be thankful that God sits high and seeks low. Our society requires a license to have a privilege or to perform certain duties here are several examples:

> You need a license to drive a car.
> You need a license to own a firearm.
> You need to be a licensed person to even direct traffic.

What people fail to realize, or don't care about is that you need a marriage license to be intimate with another person. You are doing what married people have a license to do with each other. This is for the women: don't fool yourselves. An engagement ring on your finger does not make you married or a wife, only a fiancée.

It does not make your fiancé married or a husband and your choosing to live together is a "no-no".

1 Corinthians: 6:18 (KJV) "Flee fornication. Every sin that a man doeth is without the body; but he that committeth fornication sinneth against his own body." The man gave you the ring, but he can take it back and call everything off. God forbid an unfortunate thing like this happens in the relationship. Do yourself a favor and do not get cute by saying,

"I am not giving you back the ring." You may as well because the purpose of the engagement ring is gone. It is better to end the relationship with your dignity.

This scripture talks about a devil

Revelation: 9:11 (KJV) "And they had a king over them, which is the angel of the bottomless pit, whose name in the Hebrew tongue is A-bad'don, but in the Greek tongue hath his name A-poll'yon." The truth is how can we let something other than God that doesn't have control over any dominion lead us? John: 4:24 (KJV) "God is a Spirit: and they that worship him must worship him in spirit and in truth." Whatever you do, don't lose sight of reality. Our humanness can get us into a lot of trouble. There are two I's. One is our humanism, the Ego; it is aggressive, saying, "I want this," "I want that," and is very hard to satisfy or pessimistic, saying, "I'm gonna, I'm gonna," and nothing is accomplished. We at times are unable to manage the things already received. The other side is our "I AM" or Spiritualism. God is always at peace; He does not entertain challenge(s). There are people who have faith in nonsense but only truth and faith go hand in hand. When you are faithful to God, He will put the people who can be trusted on your path. He is aware there are some trustworthy people on the planet. During the last century, a renowned Civil Rights Leader, Martin Luther King Jr. famous quotes, “Let freedom ring.” “Free at last, free at last, Thank God Almighty, were free at last!” This put hope in the hearts of men, but what are we holding on to now? The truth is one must grow in grace in order to be wiser and kinder.

Humanity misunderstood Christ during his time in this dimension. In the book of Mark: 16:19 (KJV) the latter part “he was received up into heaven, and sat on the right hand of God”.

There is a song with the following lyrics, “And I don’t want the world to see me / Cause I don’t think they’d understand / When everything’s meant to be broken / I just want you to know who I am”.

The truth is Christ will always be the freedom that humanity needs. He can free you from whatever wherever whenever and however. It is all up to you to let, “the truth make you free!”

Spiritual Warfare

Ephesians: 6:11 (KJV) "Put on the whole armour of God, that ye may be able to stand against the wiles of the devil."

Ephesians: 6:11 (AMP) "Put on God's whole armour [the armour of a heavy-armed soldier which God supplies], that you may be able successfully to stand up against [all] the strategies and the deceits of the devil."

Ephesians: 6:12 (KJV) "For we wrestle not against flesh and blood, but against principalities, against powers, against the rulers of the darkness of this world, against spiritual wickedness in high places."

Ephesians: 6:12 (AMP) "For we are not wrestling with flesh and blood [contending only with physical opponents], but against the despotisms, against the powers, against [the master spirits who are] the world rulers of this present darkness, against the spirit forces of wickedness in the heavenly (supernatural) sphere."

Spiritual Warfare

There is actually a war going on in the spirit realm that is all around us. The fight is to protect our souls from demonic forces. The carnal eyes are unable to see in the spirit realm. Only spiritual eyes are able to see in the spirit realm to fight evil spirits that must be defeated in the spirit realm. These evil forces will do one of two things: oppress or possess a person.

2 Corinthians: 10:4 (KJV) "(For the weapons of our warfare are not carnal, but mighty through God to the pulling down of strong holds;)." The eighth gift of the Holy Spirit, "divers of tongues," is one of the key ways, the anointing of this heavenly language along with a continuous praying spirit. Christ intercedes for us and our spirit remains in a perfect dwelling position prostrated at Christ's feet in the spirit realm. You can be certain demonic forces cannot hinder you "Hallelujah!"

These evil spirits are agents on assignment, and they're assigned to operate through other people. Some people lives are so chaotic that they are unable to detect they're being used by evil spirits.

They seek out a person's weakness or interest and this is part of their master plan. They are considered to be supplying your wants and needs the best thing to do is seek, God and let him move them out of your life.

The Ego and its demons are fearful because time is winding down and they're desperate. The reason why is because God's still in control.

The Ego chooses to dwell in areas that are comfortable. It is liable to do anything ungodly by operating out of willing vessels. There is a song with the following lyrics, "We've come this far by faith / leaning on the Lord / Trusting in his holy word / He's never fail me yet / Oh can't turn around / we've come this far by faith."

The believer's must follow their assignments from God to the letter. This will prevent demonic forces from overpowering us in anyway, shape, form, or fashion. Your soul has a test that cannot be ignored. Why? It is because you cannot serve two masters: God and the Ego. You will love one and hate the other it's a critical choice you have to make. When you are in the company of people and things don't feel right or are not turning out right, these people will try to convince you that you're supposed to be on the path with them. The truth is they are not on your path, but actually in your way.

There are three voices that are heard: God's, yours, and the Ego's. We are supposed to be able to discern the voice of God from any other voice.

We are God's children and are expected to be victors in spiritual warfare not victims.

"He that is in me is greater than he that is in the world." You are the head and not the tail.

We are on the battlefield for God, and nothing else matters. There is no mystery; the book of Revelation has revealed the winner: God!

Delays do not mean that the answer is no

Genesis: 21:2-3 (KJV) "For Sarah conceived, and bare Abraham a son in his old age, at the set time of which God had spoken to him. And Abraham called the name of his son that was born unto him, whom Sarah bare to him, Isaac."

Delays do not mean that the answer is no

Abraham and Sarah were old, and they thought it was impossible for her to conceive a child. God planted a seed in Sarah's womb and blessed them with a biological child. She gave birth to the promised child, Isaac. Their story demonstrates a delay according to the human mind that does not mean "no."

We all have a conscious and a subconscious God has incorporated them into our being. Our faith is designed to make a connection with the conscious and the sub-conscious during our lives. We must realize it all derives from the subconscious. There are times we have prayed and asked God for things and did not receive them immediately.

Do not get hung up on delays thinking that it means "no", you must be firm without your faith wavering. Our fear causes us to lose control and doubt God. What is happening, the person is engrossed by the unconscious mind.

The things we so desperately want in life are received by God's speed and no one else's. God made a covenant with Abraham and it was a contract sealed with his blessings. Whatever promises God made to us are also sealed in this fashion.

Some people are able to obtain what is called the "American Dream". There are both parents in the household, each with a prestigious job and lucrative incomes and children. The home has a white picket fence and two vehicles in the garage. There are others for whom this dream appears to be eons away or impossible to obtain in this life. Delays don't mean no, there are old sayings pertaining to this: "Good things come to those who wait," and "The best is yet to come." We are not perfect in our current state, but delays can remain powerless in our lives.

God Anointed, Not Self-Appointed

Luke: 4:18 &19 (KJV) "THE SPIR'IT OF THE LORD IS UPON ME, BECAUSE HE HATH ANOINTED ME TO PREACH THE GOSPEL TO THE POOR; HE HATH SENT ME TO HEAL THE BROKEN-HEARTED TO PREACH DELIVERANCE TO THE CAPTIVES, AND RECOVERING OF SIGHT TO THE BLIND, SET AT LIBERTY THEM THAT ARE BRUISED, 19 TO PREACH THE ACCEPTABLE YEAR OF THE LORD."

God Anointed, Not Self-Appointed

We are all here for a purpose and for an appointed time according to God. His plan for our life and his commandments are intertwined. We are not always entrusted with the appropriate position by the world. These positions will not only affect our lives, but others as well. Sometimes it can take one person to turn your life upside down or inside out. It cannot be stressed enough that the pastoral office is an imperative office to hold for a man or a woman. In the Book of Luke: 4:18 tells that the Holy Spirit anointed Christ to preach the gospel. The saints must be aware that not everyone in the pulpit is God-anointed; some are self-appointed. The saints come to the house of worship week after week, year after year, to receive spiritual nourishment from the Word of God. When the saints are not spiritually fed, they are left in spiritual darkness. There has been a transformation in the house of worship, it has become a booming business or somewhat secular. There is so much prestige, money, and other benefits in this arena.

The pastors of these houses of worship have to realize that they are responsible for the saints under their leadership. The saints put their trust in their pastors. Some have put more trust in their pastors than in God. It is the responsibility of the pastor to make sure he or she is instructed by God and not the Ego. It cannot be said anymore plainly; instead of being a house of worship it will become a house of confusion. It will attract Satanic Worshippers and the congregation can become susceptible to being swayed by doctrines other than the gospel of Christ. If God has not blessed you with the gift to be an under-shepherd or under-shepherdess in the kingdom, why take the chance of deceiving so many or anyone? When you deceive people, you are able to control them. God has revealed through his word that there will be false messengers. Christ was anointed to operate out of the fivefold ministry. The fivefold ministry officeholders are expected to be anointed and to bring the teachings of Christ through these offices to the saints. If you are not called by God and anointed by the Holy Spirit to enter a pulpit out of any, of these fivefold ministries please do not tempt the Lord thy God.

The Word of God is One Word.

Luke: 8:11 (KJV) “Now the parable is this: The word of God is a seed.”

The Word of God Is One Word

God has us covered in the spirit realm and in the physical realm with the one word. There are people who say the written word of God is composed of made-up stories. Do not be offended we don't pray to the written word of God. We pray to the word of God that was made flesh and dwelled among humanity. I hold on to the word of God that was made flesh because no one was able to tamper with him. All that was required was done perfectly. This is why Christ will never seek us for prayer, but we must seek Him. There is a song with the title "If You Make One Step, Jesus Will Make Two".

God and his Word are Eternal and will never lose their Power. The written word of God is supposed to match the word of God that is imprinted in the heart of man. When you read the word of God, it is supposed to connect from perfection to perfection, 360 degrees, flowing and feeding it self. These are dimensions within you introduced by the Holy Spirit. The word of God is sixty-six books written by man and translated into thousands of languages. The Bible is Basic Instructions for Believing and Living Eternally. Some of us think our pay, checks is our daily bread. The Word of God is our daily bread from heaven. The paycheck is for our bread and butter.

The word of God has codes that have not been completely decoded. There are infinite revelations in these codes.

Isaiah: 55:11 (KJV) "So shall my word be that goeth forth out of my mouth: it shall not return unto me void, but it shall accomplish that which I please, and it shall prosper in the thing whereto I sent it." God can only speak truth.

A parallel scripture Genesis: 1:3 (KJV) "And God said, Let there be light: and there was light." God commanded the light and it came forth all over the universe."

These two scriptures reveal that words are under God's authority. The omnipotence of God exists within us but it is under his control. The power of life and death is in the tongue. What we say at times can have an affect on another person. There is a saying that goes, "If you don't have anything nice to say, don't say anything at all." We cannot say or whisper a word without God knowing. Christ the crucified and resurrected one. He is written about in the New Testament the Gospels. Christ has a Face that makes the Sun, Moon, and Stars Shine. Christ performed abundant miracles in his journey on earth. He spoke one word and the sick, blind, deaf, and lame were instantly healed. This is the impact he had on humanity. God is aware we need a fresh word for a new season. The Holy Spirit will reveal it to those who preach the word of God, but the deliverance of the message will be different. What counts is the message was delivered. God had the first word in our lives and he will have the last word. Look at the parallelism of the scriptures, they bind together and become One Word. The One Word of God is Christ!

The Second Adam / The Restoration of Man

John: 1:1 (KJV) “In the beginning was the Word, and the Word was with God, and the Word was God”.

John: 1:14 (KJV) “And the Word was made flesh, and dwelt among us, (and we beheld his glory, the glory as of the only begotten of the Father,) full of grace and truth”.

The Second Adam / The Restoration of Man

The grace of God is Christ (God's riches at Christ's expense). The lost sheep were not aware God had chosen them out of humanity. Christ was designated here to change their lives forever. The transformation was simple and only required them to have faith in him. Christ said, "Believe in me." Their faith would allow a relationship to be established. The people were supposed to see Christ and focus. This was a test of the spirit to the spirit. Their disbelief and the fear within their hearts prevented the transformation and they rejected Christ.

Matthew: 4:1(KJV) "Then was Jesus led up of the Spirit into the wilderness to be tempted of the devil." Christ was tested before his ministry began. The temptation of Christ took place on three levels as well. The first level of temptation was weakness in the flesh; the second was materialism and the last level was the extent of power. The omnipotence of God in Christ can resist any temptation on the earth and we're expected to do the same. What led to Christ's crucifixion? He did not come wearing a white robe with wings and riding on a white horse. He came in flesh, like humanity did and walked the earth which made it difficult for the people to believe. Although Christ's teachings were very simple they were far beyond the understanding of any of the Pharisees, Chief-Priests or Scribes. We must remember this was the Word giving the word to describe his father's ways through the parables. Christ explained that his kingdom was not of this world; if it had been, his servants would have fought to keep him from being handed to the Jews. Christ had the audacity to perform miracles even on the Sabbath, which was considered breaking the law. Christ came in flesh and blood and was beaten before going to the cross. Their belief was if he bleeds, he can be killed. Let us look at the parallelism between the two Adams. The first Adam was in the Garden of Eden. The second Adam was in the Garden of Gethsemane. The garden is the place where both Adams made significant decisions for humanity. The first Adam resided in tranquility (heaven); he made a decision through his free will that caused him to fall away from God. The second Adam, in his servant position, was not vulnerable at all and fulfilled God's will. We take his grace for granted so imagine dealing with the Old Testament God on a regular basis. Whatever humanity sowed negatively, He allowed the punishment to be swift and appropriately. The disobedient act takes place on several levels of your life. The punishment will also affect several levels of your life.

The imperative questions that will be asked after your journey has ended in this realm are "Did you live for God?" and "What did you do for God?"

While on the cross during the crucifixion, Christ opened the invisible door. He is waiting for all to walk through to where Love, Light, and Truth await them. This door is still open today within you and all around you. When the pastor says, "The doors of the church are open." You are coming with an open and humble heart and walking through the invisible door of infinity, of Christ.

Christ said "I knock at the door." The door he is referring to is the heart of man, where the Holy Spirit—speaks to man in a, still soft voice. Christ knocking on the door of your heart is inspiring you to come through the invisible door.

When Christ said those three significant words, "It is finished!", the masses were mentally unable to reach the level to comprehend these key words. Christ was saying that sin, sickness, and death—all of the curses the first Adam was subjected to—would no longer exist in this realm. The world's way of thinking and living was finished.

Christ revealed during the crucifixion that He is the sacrificial lamb. You are eternally blessed through his blood that gave eternal life. The unbelievable would become believable.

Christ is the Eternal, Universal, Perfect, Being.

What happened? They continuously miss Christ. Our circumstances are still serious. After Christ's crucifixion, the Roman soldiers finally believed that Christ was the

Son of God. What Christ did on the cross was the "greatest good" for all!

Matthew: 15: 18, 19 & 20 (KJV) "But those things which proceed out of the mouth come forth from the heart; and they defile the man. 19 For out of the heart proceed evil thoughts, murders, adulteries, fornications, thefts, false witness, blasphemies":

20 These are the things which defile a man: but to eat with unwashen hands defileth not a man."

He came from heaven into the world time man's unconsciousness. Sometimes it can take one life to save others.

The Oneness of God and Your Oneness with God

John: 14:10-12 (KJV) "Believest thou not that I am in the Father, and the Father in me? the word that I speak unto you I speak not of myself: but the Father that dwelleth in me, he doeth the works.

11 Believe me that I am in the Father, and the Father in me: or else believe me for the very works' sake.

12 Verily, verily, I say unto you, He that believeth on me, the works that I do shall he do also, and greater works than these shall he do; because I go unto my father".

John: 17:1, 7-8, 11 (KJV) These words spake Jesus, and lifted up his eyes to heaven, and said, "Father, the hour is come; glorify thy Son, that thy Son also may glorify thee.

7 Now they have known that all things whatsoever thou hast givest me are of thee.

8 For I have given unto them the words which thou gavest me; and they have received them, and have known surely that I came out from thee, and they have believed that thou didst send me.

11 And now I am no more in the world, but these are in the world, and I come to thee. Holy Father, keep through thine own name those whom thou hast given me, that they may be one as we are".

John: 17:21-23,26 (KJV) "That they all may be one; as thou, Father, art in me, and I in thee, that they also may be one in us: that the world may believe that thou hast sent me.

22 And the glory which thou gavest me I have given them; that they may be one, even as we are one:

23 I in them, and thou in me, that they may be made perfect in one; and that the world may know that thou hast sent me, and hast loved them, as thou hast loved me.

26 And I have declared unto them thy name, and will declare it: that the love wherewith thou hast loved me may be in them, and I in them".

The Oneness of God and Your Oneness with God

There are several names for the three persons of God: The Trinity, the God-Head, or the Tribune.

In the Book of Matthew: 3:16 talks about what happened when Jesus was baptized, He went straight up out of the water and the heavens were opened over him, and the Spirit of God descending like a dove, and lighting on him.

This is the baptismal formula; it is baptizing the people in the name of the Father, the first person who spoke; the Mother, the Holy Spirit, the second person descending like a dove from above; and the Son, the third person, who was standing in the water.

Once you go down into the water, the old person has gone and a new person rises from the water. The light of God is revealed through you. There is a song with a lyric that explains who Jesus is "Jesus, the Light of the World."

Genesis: 6:6 explained how God himself experienced hurt before going to the cross, because He regretted making mankind. What is known as the flood took place and it caused his heart to grieve because unconditional Love cannot fade away. In the book of Matthew: 27:46 (HBAET) "And about the ninth hour, Jesus cried out with a loud voice and said, Eli, Eli, lemana shabakthani!" This means, My God, my God, for this I was spared!" Christ did not say,

"My God, my God, why hast thou forsaken me?" Why would Christ need to call a fleet of angels? Christ was God in flesh on the cross.

God is always with us because he's Spirit with the ability to go and to see beyond flesh. The realm we're residing in is actually eternity. I know that it is difficult to understand or to believe but God can reveal it if you just let him. Humanity was sent out of eternity into eternity.

Children at a tender age they're able to see and hear angels speak. It is unfortunate that our crown charka will seal up at a certain age. When a male child is under three years of age, we recommend that his hair is not cut before he's three. The mold of the head has to be closed to prevent a delay in his ability to speak. When we transform in life the crown charka has to open up. This will give us the ability to clearly hear God speaking to us. God is definitely able to hear our prayers we should always end the prayer by saying, "In the name of Christ," this is actually sealing the prayer.

We have an Eternal Father; the Eternal Mother; the Holy Spirit and the Son, the Lord Christ.

One of the most important things you can do is thank them for sharing, their Eternal Oneness and Eternal Peace with us.

The Will of God

Genesis: 1:3 (KJV) "And God said, Let there be light: and there was light".

Genesis: 1:26 (KJV) "And God said, Let us make man in our image, after our likeness: and let them have dominion over the fish of the sea, and over the fowl of the air, and over the cattle, and over all the earth, and over every creeping thing that creepeth upon the earth"

Luke: 19:40 (AMP) "He replied, I tell you that if these keep silent, the very stones will cry out." A parallel scripture,

Habakkuk: 2:11 (AMP) "For the stones shall cry out of the wall [built in sin, to accuse you], and the beam out of the woodwork will answer it [agreeing with its charge against you]." It is God's will that everything that has breath praise the Lord. *Hallelujah* is the holiest, highest praise given unto God.

The Will of God

Your body is the temple of the Holy Spirit and you are expected, to care for it by eating a proper diet, exercising, and getting rest. All of this works together for the well-being of your body.

I read two health books in the early nineties that were a part of a series. These two books each had a diet to go by that would keep you in good health. It told you how to transform your way of, eating and to have a balanced diet. You would be amazed of the food that should not be eaten. The food that is very harsh on the digestive system and not digested properly. They are not eliminated from your body in a timely manner and can poison your system. A person's failure to be conscious of the food put in the body is the cause of so many deaths. There is a saying, "You are what you eat" and your unhealthy eating is a form of self-elimination.

We became the Will of God and are always going to be. God ordained that it is his will for man to have dominion over all other creations. When we look at Joseph's life, he was not only the will of God willed into existence. He also allowed the Will of God to operate through him. Joseph abundantly received the favor of God in his life and everything he touched prospered. There is nothing in this universe that can out do God because He is perfect. There is no one or nothing that can do to us, through us, or for us like God.

Matthew: 26:41 (KJV) "Watch and pray, that ye enter not into temptation: the spirit indeed is willing, but the flesh is weak." It is God's will that we keep his commandments. There are times in our lives when situations arise, and we can see exactly how to resolve them by doing x, y, and z. This will not affect anyone negatively. However, God can instead command for the situation to be resolved by doing a, b, and c. It is in our best interest to trust him. In the book of Daniel tells the story of Shadrach, Meshach, and Abednego. These three men would not worship the golden image that King Nebuchadnezzar built. Shadrach, Meshach, and Abednego were doing the Will of God. Nebuchadnezzar commanded the mighty men of his army to bind them and cast them into the fiery furnace. These three men showed no fear. There was a fourth man in the fiery furnace, awaiting them. They suffered no burns or smoke inhalation it is usually what kills a person.

Acts: 17:28 (KJV) "For in him we live, and move, and have our being; as certain also of your own poets have said, For we are also his offspring." God has expressed this through the sixty-six books of the Bible.

God's Will was designed for us to comprehend and obey here, because we're aware that His Will is the only that exist in Heaven. Where there is life, there is hope; this is the Will of God. Whatever we do in life it's God's will that He be glorified.

If anyone is uncomfortable in their flesh, I am happy. This is food for your spirit, not for your flesh.

The Kingdom of God

Matthew: 4:17 (KJV) "From that time Jesus began to preach, and to say, Repent for the kingdom of heaven is at hand."

Matthew: 4:17 (AMP) "From the time Jesus began to preach crying out, repent (change your mind for the better, heartily amend your ways, with abhorrence of your past sins), for the kingdom of heaven is at hand."

Matthew: 6:33 (KJV) "But seek ye first the kingdom of God, and his righteousness; and all these things shall be added unto you."

Luke: 19:11 (KJV) "And as they heard these things, he added and spake a parable, because he was nigh to Jerusalem, and they thought that the kingdom of God should immediately appear."

John: 18:36 (KJV) "Jesus answered, My kingdom is not of this world, then would my servants fight that I should not be delivered to the Jews: but now is my kingdom not from hence."

The Kingdom of God

Where is the kingdom of God? Genesis: 1:26 (KJV) "And God said, Let us make man in our image, after our likeness: and let them have dominion over the fish of the sea, and over the fowl of the air, and over the cattle, and over all the earth, and over every creeping thing that creepeth upon the earth."

Ezekiel: 37:4, 7, 9-10, & 12 explained the valley of dry bones. God had commanded Ezekiel to prophesy over the dry bones and bring them back to life. The bones were all connected and flesh was formed on them.

Ezekiel prophesied unto the wind to come and breathe upon those slain that they might live.

We begin with the mind of man, the ability to think and imagine. When man imagines, portals open to develop and create things in the physical realm. The thoughts of man are significant like his faith. Man's thoughts and faith go hand in hand and the wisdom lies here. The eyes are in the spirit realm on one level and the physical realm on another; this creates dual vision.

The ears are designed to listen to the stillness. It is also being swift to listen and receive a Word of Wisdom, Word of Knowledge or an extensive revelation.

The mouth is designed to speak the word of God and also prophesy prosperity into our lives; this is the Holy Spirit's spiritual gift of prophecy. The heart of man is where God has imprinted his word. The word of God is the rhythm of man in truth. The hands of man can heal sickness by touching. The Holy Spirit's spiritual; gifts of healing. The feet of man are directed to walk on the road of righteousness.

Luke: 17:20-21 (KJV) "And when he was demanded of the Pharisees, when the kingdom of God should come, he answered them and said, The kingdom of God cometh not with observation:

21 Neither shall they say, Lo here! or, lo there! for, behold, the kingdom of God is within you."

Luke: 17:20-21(AMP) "Asked by the Pharisees when the kingdom of God would come, He replied to them by saying, the kingdom of God does not come with signs to be observed or with visible display,
21 Nor will people say, look! Here [it is]! or, See, [it is] there! For behold, the kingdom of God is within you [in your hearts] and among you [surrounding you]."

Your spiritual path will fit the door to enter the kingdom perfectly revealing you were always in the kingdom.

This is one of God's attribute's Omnipresence. God and his Kingdom are one.

When revelations are revealed it is like peeling an infinite onion that continuously unveils God from the depths of his being truth.

The new heaven and new earth are one. I will reiterate the latter part of Luke: 17:21(AMP) "the kingdom of God is within you [in your hearts] and among you [surrounding you]."

What are you waiting for? Just enjoy the presence of the Holy One, his eternalness within you and all around you.

The Nature of God

John: 4:24 (KJV) "God is a Spirit: and they that worship him must worship him in spirit and in truth."

John: 4:24 (AMP) "God is a Spirit (a spirit Being) and those who worship Him must worship Him in spirit and in truth (reality)."

The Nature of God

God and the Holy Spirit are both Spirits; it is their nature. Although the spirit of God operates through flesh, it will operate at another level. It is through the spiritual gifts, they fulfill the purpose their designed to do.

Matthew: 3:16 (KJV) "And Jesus, when he was baptized, went up straightway out of the water: and, lo, the heavens were opened unto him, and he saw the Spirit of God descending like a dove, and lighting upon him." Christ was anointed for all nine spiritual gifts to be utilized through him.

The word of wisdom, the word of knowledge, the gift of faith, the gifts of healing, the working of miracles, the gift of prophecy, the discernment of spirits, the gift of speaking in tongues, the gift of the interpretation of tongues. The King James Version of the Bible, here is an illustration of the Holy Spirit's Spiritual Gifts.

1. The Word of Wisdom—Matthew: 26:21 & 23 (KJV) "And as they did

eat, he said, Verily I say unto you, that one of you shall betray me. 23 And he answered and said, He that dippeth his hand with me in the dish, the same shall betray me."

2. The Word of Knowledge—John: 4:13-14 (KJV) "Jesus answered and said unto her, Whosoever drinketh of this water shall thirst again:
   14 But whosoever drinketh the water that I shall give him shall never thirst; but the water that I shall give him shall be in him a well of water springing up into everlasting life."

3. The Gift of Faith—Matthew: 9:20 & 22 (KJV) "And, behold, a woman, which was diseased with an issue of blood twelve years, came behind him, and touched the hem of his garment:
   22 But Jesus turned him about, and when he saw her, he said, Daughter, be of good comfort; thy faith hath made thee whole. And the woman was made whole from that hour."

Matthew: 14:26 (KJV) Christ had to have faith to walk on the sea.

4. The Gifts of Healing—Matthew: 9:35 (KJV) "Jesus went about preaching the gospel and healing every sickness and every disease that the people suffered."

5. The Working of Miracles—Matthew: 14:17&19 (KJV) "And they say unto him, We have here but five loaves, and two fishes".
   19 And he commanded the multitude to sit down on the grass, and took the five loaves, and the two fishes, and looking up to heaven, he blessed, and brake, and gave the loaves to his disciples, and the disciples to the multitude."

6. The Gift of Prophecy
   John: 2:19 (KJV) "Jesus answered and said unto them, Destroy this temple, and in three days I will raise it up."

7. The Discernment of Spirit John: 1:32 (KJV) "And John bare record, saying, I

saw the Spirit descending from heaven like a dove, and it abode upon him."

8. The Gift of Speaking in tongues—Matthew: 27:46 (HBAET) "And about the ninth hour, Jesus cried out with a loud voice and said, Eli, Eli lemana shabakthan!"

9. The Gift of the Interpretation of tongues was demonstrated in Matthew: 27:46. (HBAET) This is the interpretation of what Christ spoke in tongues: "My God, my God, for this I was spared!" 1 This was my destiny."

The Holy Spirit's spiritual gifts correspond with our five senses.

Sight—seeing the wondrous miracles that are performed by the Holy Spirit
Hearing—the still, soft voice that speaks to and guide us;
Touch—the gentle touch to which nothing on earth can compare
Smell—the Holy Spirit comes with a sweet fragrance

Taste—the bitterness in your heart will vanish

The nature of God, the Eternal Spirit, is Life, Love, Light, Truth, Heaven, Joy, Peace, Omnipresence, Omniscience, Omnipotence, and Immutability! All of these, bind together is Him; Love is Radiating from His Being.

The nine spiritual gifts of the Holy Spirit are nine levels and they bind together to become One.

Fear in the Church

Genesis: 37:5, 9-10 (KJV) "And Joseph dreamed a dream and he told it his brethren: and they hated him yet the more. And he dreamed yet another dream and told it his brethren, and said, Behold, I have dreamed a dream more; and behold, the sun and the moon and the eleven stars made obeisance to me. And he told it to his father, and to his brethren: and his father rebuked him, and said to him, What is this dream that thou hast dreamed? Shall I and thy mother and thy brethren indeed come to bow down ourselves to thee to earth?"

Fear in the Church

Joseph had a dream and revealed it to his brothers. However he did not realize the extent of hate in their hearts for him. Some Church members are deliberately cloaking a spirit of fear toward one another. What the Church has failed to realize is only God can put a calling on a person's life. This calling has to be ordained by him. The Church is expected to behave differently from others. You accepted Christ as your Lord and Savior and He is due the respect.

There are others who did not take the step of faith or attempt to make the commitment.

Fear in the church is prevalent when you have members in the church for, several decades. Their belief is a change will not be beneficial for the church. You cannot keep doing things the same way and, expect different results. God is not in the mess-blessing business. They fear others using their gifts it suppose to edify the church. Fear is the underlying root that envy, jealousy, anger and selfishness stem from and it's manifested in the church. God has new people who are not traditional hoarders. The question is why do you fear someone else's gifts, or anointing?

You do not realize the extent of your, conduct when you start minding God's business. You have the audacity to think you know more than God.

God is omniscient, which means He knows all. You think God does not see you? He's omnipresent He is everywhere, even inside of you. You consider this behavior to be a Christian walk. You may think I am being too judgmental. I would rather have someone tell me the truth than to continue sowing seeds of fear and reap the harvest.

We need to fear that God is not hearing our prayers and make them sincere. God is not a man to lie or a god of fear.

When he has put a ministry in you, at the appointed time, it will be fulfilled. It will be as though he parted the Red Sea for you to pass through. There will always be potential pastors. God knows that the spirit is willing, so keep your flesh in alignment with the spirit.

Matthew: 9:37-38 Christ explained to the disciples that the harvest has plenty, but there are few laborers. He instructed them to pray to the Lord of the harvest that he expeditiously sent laborers into the harvest. When it comes to pastoring, they're not entrusted with the same amount of members. There are different techniques of pastoring some are teachers and others are preachers.

You also have different forms of preparation. Some people were directed by God to attend school. There are others who were born with the word of God in their mouth and taught by the Holy Spirit. These are words of wisdom. Whoever you are stop fearing; let go and let God!

Stay in Your Place

1 Peter: 5:6 (KJV) "Humble yourselves therefore under the mighty hand of God, that he may exalt you in due time:"

1 Peter: 5:6 (AMP) "Therefore humble yourselves [demote, lower yourselves in your own estimation] under the mighty hand of God, that in due time He may exalt you."

Stay in Your Place

It is staying under the direction of God. We should accept and enjoy what God has planned in this journey for us. However there are people who will come into your life and try to make you fall in your conscious. It is done by wiping out your conscious and projecting their idea(s) on you. Do not let people rent your mind or energy because you are focusing on them instead of God. Stay within the kingdom of God do, not venture outside looking for the answers. Stay in your place as though there; is no other place that exist. We all have an Ego, but some of us rely on it more than others.

Do not let your Ego or someone else's, be your god because it will lead to unconscionable decisions. Do not sow seeds or allow anyone else to sow seeds that are tares in your garden. Your garden will be like the unfruitful fig tree Christ cursed. A person must be careful of who is giving them information. Everyone who says God sent them was not sent by him. They have ulterior motives and will use information as an excuse to get to you. They come to you because they are in need and are users. They're attempting to make your life worse than theirs. These people are victims of their own poor judgment and want you to be a victim as well. What actually happens is it comes back on them like a boomerang and the universe has perfect aim.

This is referring to Genesis: 6:2,4 (KJV) "That the sons of God saw the daughters of men that they were fair; and they took them wives of all which they chose.

4 There were giants in the earth in those days; and also after that, when the sons of God came in unto the daughters of men, and they bare children to them, the same became mighty men which were of old, men of renown."

These angels did not stay on their assignment from God; in other words, they didn't stay in their domain. They fell and became spiritually lost. When you mix ungodliness with godliness, the results will be chaotic.

Galatians: 6:9 (KJV) "And let us not be weary in well doing: for in due season we shall reap, if we faint not." When God is in agreement with your conduct, it will be as though God has prepared a table for you in the presence of your enemies. The reward is returning to you a hundredfold. Let's look at the behavior of the children of Israel for example. Moses was assigned by God to deliver the chosen people out of bondage. They chose not to stay in their place in faith by not trusting God. The children of Israel allowed their hearts to be tested by occurrences in life.

It caused fear to get in the way of their faithful journey. It is unfortunate that God's chosen people continued to fall short of his glory. At this time one of the imperative ways it can happen is some people, will use the Bible and twist it to justify the corrupt decisions they make and this can mislead you. You must use the wisdom God gave you and the spirit of discernment in order to receive your own revelation. In the Book of Matthew: 20:1-16 tells the story of the workers in the vineyard. The vineyard represents our life experience. Once you took the penny, you signed a treaty and agreed to live your life according to God's plan. The significant verse is 16 and it states, "So the last shall be first, and the first last: for many be called, but few chosen." There are two points explicitly explained in verse 16.

> Every one of the hired laborers agreed to work for a penny a day and was rewarded equally.
>
> Some of the hired laborers criticized the householder because of the hand dealt to them.

We must look at ourselves, because the question lies within us. Did I agree to do better in order to receive better? This question is hypothetical regarding humanity. We are all the same in the eyes of our eternal father.

2 Peter:3:8 (KJV) "But, beloved, be not ignorant of this one thing, that one day is with the Lord as a thousand years, and a thousand years as one day." We are only here for a second in the eyes of God it is how you want to label it. Once you agreed to the plan, agreement, or contract with God,

the next breath was in this dimension. It might look as though the plan, agreement, or contract that God made with someone else has more favor or flavor than yours. You must see yours for what God really designed it to be.

We are all under God's order, whether it is understood or not. We are supposed to stick to the plan, agreement, or contract God made with each of us. At some point, we lose focus and live according to our free will. Let us look at Adam and Eve in the garden. Adam was directly told by God not to "eat" from the tree of the knowledge of good and evil. Eve took from the tree, ate and she did not change. When she gave it to Adam and he ate, life for humanity completely changed. What is one man's poison can be another man's cure. Our experiences are different, but the destination has to be the same; back to "Papa's house."

Matthew: 25:15-29 discusses the talents. The servant with five talents earned an additional five talents. His reward was ruler over many things. The servant with the two talents earned an additional two talents. His reward was also ruler over many things. The servant with the one talent failed to use it and did not earn an additional talent. The servant with the one talent did not trust God in order for his will to be fulfilled through him regarding the one talent. All he needed was faith the size of a mustard seed with the one talent. His reward could have been ruler over things exceedingly. At the end of this journey called life, we will go back to our eternal father. He will review our deed(s). Were they on the mark, or did they totally miss it? God is the decision maker. Revelation: 7:17 (KJV) "For the lamb which is in the midst of the throne shall feed them, and shall lead them unto living fountains of waters: and God shall wipe away all tears from their eyes." God does not abandon any of his children.

He comes to us through other people as well and gives us a message. Their failure to listen to God made life very disappointing, as well as painful. You don't want people results, you want God results. Staying in your place is like being a watchtower. You are fleshed and clothed and able to be in your spirit. When you stay in your place, you are staying on post within yourself waiting for the bridegroom; Christ.

The Mysteries of the Kingdom of God

Mark: 4:10-13 (KJV) "And when he was alone, they that were about him with the twelve asked of him the parable.

11And he said unto them, Unto you it is given to know the mystery of the kingdom of God: but unto them that are without, all these things are done in parables:

12 THAT SEEING THEY MAY SEE, AND NOT PERCEIVE; AND HEARING THEY MAY HEAR, AND NOT UNDERSTAND; LEST AT ANY TIME THEY SHOULD BE CONVERTED AND THEIR SINS SHOULD BE FORGIVEN THEM.

13 And he said unto them, know ye not this parable? and how then will ye know all parables?"

Mark: 4:10-13 (AMP)"And as soon as He was alone, those who were around Him, with the Twelve [apostles], began to ask Him about the parables.
11 And He said To them, to you has been entrusted the mystery of the kingdom of God [that is, the secret counsels of God which are hidden from the ungodly]; but for those outside [of the circle] everything becomes a parable.
12 In order that they may [indeed] look and look but not see and perceive, and may hear and hear but not grasp and comprehend lest haply they should not turn again, and it [their willful rejection of the truth] should be forgiven them.

13 And He said to them, Do you not discern and understand this parable?" "How then is it possible for you to discern and understand all the parables?"

The Mysteries of the Kingdom of God

When you receive a revelation, God is actually speaking to you. However everyone is not ready to receive God's revelations beyond the parables. God, through his attribute of omniscience is aware of our belief or disbelief. God will not force truth on us. When you look through the Gospels, you can see that the ultimate mystery of the kingdom of God is Christ. The Pharisees, Chief-Priests, Scribes, and the Masses did not see him as a supernatural being. Christ was a rabble-rouser and a blasphemer in the eyes of the Pharisees, Chief-Priests and Scribes; he could not be tolerated. The mystery was Christ giving himself up to the people and put on the cross according to our Eternal Family. Christ, the fisher of souls, chose twelve souls to be his disciples. There are secret societies in the world, but their practices may not glorify God at all. The church is not a secret society, but they are expected to be separate from others like the children of Israel.

I will reiterate Mark: 4:11, "And he said unto them, Unto you it is given to know the mysteries of the kingdom of God: but unto them that are without, all these things are done in parables."

Christ had an inner circle within his inner circle. The twelve disciples were Christ's inner circle.

The inner circle within was composed of Peter, James and John. These three went with him into the Garden of Gethsemane and witnessed the transfiguration. Christ's face shone like the sun, and his raiment was as white as light.

Luke: 10:23-24 (KJV) "And he turned him unto his disciples, and said privately, Blessed are the eyes which see the things that ye see:

24 For I tell you, that many prophets and kings have desired to see those things which ye see, and have not seen them; and to hear those things which ye hear, and have not heard them."

The disciples received the mysteries of the kingdom of God through Christ revealing himself.

1Timothy: 3:9 (KJV) "Holding the mystery of the faith in a pure conscience."

The disciples were instructed to continue spreading the gospel of Christ without revealing the mysteries.

The mysteries of the kingdom of God will be revealed to his chosen ones in this generation. The mysteries of the kingdom are precious jewels and are not to be mocked. The mysteries of the kingdom of God are also his facets.

Galatians: 3:28 (KJV) "There is neither Jew nor Greek, there is neither bond nor free, there is neither male nor female: for ye are all one in Christ Jesus."

A mystery of the kingdom of God that plagues humanity is "what happens". When our love ones make their transition into the invisible realm, we believe they are in heaven. Where they are exactly and what, they're doing is unknown to us. They have entered another state of consciousness. We believe our love ones are resting or maybe worshipping him continuously.

John: 4:24 (KJV) "God is a Spirit: and they that worship him must worship him in spirit and in truth." What has been revealed to us is we don't die. Wherever your destination is you will be conscious, in reference to experiencing the circumstances. As you can see God through his unconditional love revealed some vital information through the parables for the masses. It was a way to enlighten them as well. The mysteries of the kingdom of God bind together to become one mystery: God's Wisdom.

The Importance of the Now

Exodus: 3:14 (KJV) "And God said unto Moses, I AM THAT I AM: and he said, Thus shalt thou say unto the children of Israel, I AM hath sent me unto you."
Exodus: 3:14 (AMP) "And God said to Moses, I AM WHO I AM and WHAT I AM, and I WILL BE WHAT I WILL BE: and He said, You shall say this to the Israelites: I AM has sent me to you!"

The definition of *now* is "at the present time or the current moment." God is ever present.

The Importance of the Now

God revealed himself as the "Now" to Moses in Exodus: 3:14 because this is God's Existence. Humanity is experiencing this journey in three stages, past, present and future. However some things in the past can be stuck in your mind, but you must not allow yourself to relive the situations. Do not go through life thinking about what you should have, would have, or could have done. What is done is done, so move on with your life. The present always exist, and God is asking that you follow him "Now." He was saying, "Come out of the world "Now." The human mind tries to calculate God according to time. The infiniteness of God goes hand in hand with the now eternity.

The second spiritual gift of the Holy Spirit is the Word of Knowledge it operates in the (Now) with no past or future. God's attribute of omnipresence means He exists everywhere now. As long as the omnipresence of God is in your being and all around you, you are always in the now (him). Once you are aware of the "Now" inside of you, the now can make all things possible according to the Now.

Matthew: 26:41 (KJV) "Watch and pray, that ye enter not into temptation: the spirit indeed is willing, but the flesh is weak." We want things to happen in our time. We must realize the "Now" with God does not coincide with the now of our flesh.

John: 10:11 (KJV), "I am the good shepherd:" John: 10:36 (KJV), I am the Son of God"; John: 11:25 (KJV), "I am the resurrection and the life," John: 14:6 (KJV), "I am the way, the truth, and the life:" and John: 15:1(KJV), "I am the true vine, and my Father is the husbandman."

Christ is our Lord and Savior, he is all of the above titles and others not mentioned. I talked earlier about the past; we hold on to it as though there is nothing else. There are things that have happened to us during our childhood. We had no control over these situations.

There are times you may have caused unnecessary situations and you now view with regret. What has to be observed are they affecting our lives now regarding not being healed? The sad part is some people have never begun the healing process. The situation may have been more painful, in some cases than others. There is healing in the spirit realm waiting only for you, so open up and receive it. On a positive note, some people receive the healing in their lifetime. There is an expression that goes, "If I knew then what I know now." There is the possibility that life may have been a whole lot different in terms of experiences. The now-ness is your ultimate place in the universe, because now has an effect on every second of your life.

There is a song with the following lyrics, "The Lord is blessing me right now / He woke me up this morning and started me on my way". We don't die as long as the breath of God is in us. It's whether you woke up on this side of the "Jordan River" or on the other side, God still woke you up and said, "Go forth now and be according to my will." God is still your now-ness wherever you are.

When Christ performed miracles in this realm, he commanded that they be done now. He dwelled in the Now even during His Crucifixion. This is the importance of the now.

Humanity has allowed the world to be its all and all. The world now is a battlefield upon which there is a war between good and evil.

This is why Christ wants us to believe in him "Now" and he will only be received. Whatever has you bound, let him remove it now so there will be no crosses to carry or to bear. We see the importance of the now that humanity has lost its grip in this realm. Humanity must make a decision now to choose God or the world.

There are people who have gone through a near transition experience. During the experience they were able to understand everything. When they returned to this physical level of the now, things were readjusted. Due to their leap of experience into the invisible now that is in reference to our perception. There is an invisible line between the visible now and the invisible now. Once you receive the invisible, the invisible line is removed and things become visible.

Do not try to change your now; embrace it and allow God to continue bringing your ordained Now-ness.

The importance of the now is we can say: I am who I am in God Forever, More Now". . .

God Hide Me in Your Heart

Hebrews: 6:18 (AMP) "This was so that, by two unchangeable things [His promise and his oath] in which it is impossible for God ever to prove false or deceive us, we who have fled [to Him] for refuge might have mighty indwelling strength and strong encouragement to grasp and hold fast the hope appointed for us and set before [us]."

The Merriam Webster Dictionary defines the heart as it refers to the whole personality, the emotional or moral part of a person, as distinguished from the intellectual nature; it is also courage and one's inner being.

God Hide Me in Your Heart

"God, hide me in your heart." What does that really mean? The key word is *heart*. What comes to mind are these simple words for a short prayer: "God, hide me in your heart." God, you know where it starts. You know where the deepest emotions lie within my heart. You are the designer of the heart and fashioned it to operate with unconditional love. We are supposed to let you orchestrate the heart as well throughout life, it's sharing the heart of God. It is revealed in the two greatest commandments. However there are people who commit crimes, such as rape or murder.

Do not hate the sinner, but hate the sin; it is how God views us. This behavior reveals the separation that took place because of the fall of man. God sought the hearts of the people and found one man. In the Book of Acts: 13:22 describes what God saw in David: "DAVID the son of Jesse, A MAN AFTER MINE OWN HEART, which shall fulfill my will." David was the heart of the matter when it came to God.

God, hide me in your heart where love, peace, and joy will engulf me eternally. God allows us to look deep within our own heart to see what is not seen by others. "God, hide me in your heart." Although humanity has tried to con God with false promises, it is a true blessing to know that nothing can deceive the heart of God. God has a universal heart with the ability to identify sincerity. "God, hide me in your heart." Why not want to dwell there in the here and now and the hereafter? You have gained access to the right place God's heart. The treasures and fruits of heaven are at your disposal. They are there to rejuvenate you continuously—spiritually, mentally, and physically.

God, hide me in your heart, the ultimate place of sanctuary in the universe. God is the Eternal resting place for humanity.

Falling in Your Faith in God

Luke: 21:26 (KJV) "Men's hearts failing them for fear, and for looking after those things which are coming on the earth: for the power of heaven shall be shaken."

Romans: 14:23 (KJV) "And he that "doubteth" is damned if he eat, because he eateth not of faith: for whatever is not of faith is sin."

Romans: 14:23 (AMP) "But the man who has doubts (misgivings, an uneasy conscience) about eating, and then eats [perhaps because of you], stands condemned [before God], because he is not true to his convictions and he does not act from faith. For whatever does not originate and proceed from faith is sin [whatever is done without a conviction of its approval by God is sinful]."

1Timothy: 4:1 (KJV) "NOW THE Spirit speaketh expressly, that in the latter times some shall depart from the faith, giving heed to seducing spirits, and doctrines of devils."

1Timothy: 4:1 (AMP) "BUT THE [Holy] Spirit distinctly and expressly declares that in latter times some will turn away from the faith, giving attention to deluding and seducing spirits and doctrines that demons teach."

The word *faith* in the Merriam Webster Dictionary defines it as the following: "allegiance to duty or a person: loyalty; belief and trust in God; complete trust; a system of religious beliefs." Now, let's look at the word *falling*: to descend freely by the force of gravity; to lower, to become lowered; drop; to commit an immoral act; to pass from one condition to another; fall from grace: backslide and fall short; to be deficient.

Falling in Your Faith in God

When you look at your life, faith can have an effect on it. There are two questions: Who do you believe in? What do you believe in? Humanity can be very inconsistent in these areas. Why? Because you can initially have all the faith in the world for believing whatever you're, believing in. However one word that is contradictory can change your whole out look. As a result you will feel like a fool for believing in the people or things. I want to show two examples that we have more faith in man than in God. One we go to work everyday and it is under a contract that the Government, State, City or Private Company we're employed at will pay us every two weeks. We purchase merchandise from companies online or magazines using a credit card or a debt card trusting that no one else obtains the card number and use it. In addition the merchandise will be delivered to our residence. These are common transactions however everyone doesn't have faith to pay tithes.

There is such a thing as negative faith people that deliberately wish for the worst.

They are only focused on the negative things in life and afraid to step out on faith. You must allow yourself to become one with positive faith. There are two questions one must ask oneself: Am I able to handle what I see? Am I wearing the garment that God designed for me?

Why sin? The time you are taking out to ask God for forgiveness, you could be praising and thanking him for his goodness. One of Christ's disciples, Thomas, was well known for his doubting about Christ's resurrection. We can fall into the Doubting Thomas syndrome and dwell there for weeks, years or maybe even a lifetime. One of the most severe doubts is self-doubt this is very unhealthy and it, can cause depression and lead to other illnesses within your being. Do not let your faithlessness be a thorn in your side. It is being your own worst enemy. When your faith is low, this can be a critical time. It is more than likely your judgment will be clouded so do not make any major or quick decisions. The only major or quick decision that should be made is using kneeology go to God in prayer. We must make it a practice;

do not let the sun go down and you are still doubting God. The level of faith that Shadrach, Meshach, and Abednego had in God could not be suppressed. We should not walk around on this planet faithless.

In the Book of John: 3:16 (KJV) tells us "For God so loved the world, that he gave his only begotten Son, that whosoever believeth in him shall not perish, but have everlasting life." This is the ultimate test of faith, believing that Christ died on the cross for humanity.

Put yourself in God's hands

Matthew: 6:33 (KJV) "But seek ye, first the kingdom of God, and his righteousness; and all these things shall be added unto you."

Matthew: 6:33 (AMP) "But seek (aim at and strive after) first of all His kingdom and His righteousness (His way of doing and being right), and then these things taken together will be given you besides."

Put Yourself in God's hands

We had an infinite level of trust in God to agree to come and dwell in this dimension called earth. You are in the hands of the potter God. It is His Will that you allow yourself to be transformed back into a celestial being.

Christ has paved the way for us to believe and receive. Christ did not only come to set the captives free on earth. There were people who had passed on before the crucifixion and did not receive salvation. His purpose for going to Hell, as stated in Acts: 2:31, was to set them free. While in hell they suffered no torment they were asleep. This is the fairness of God, giving them salvation as well. It is said that Christ also took the keys of death and hell. These keys came into effect after the fall of man. They say that truth is not for the masses who, are told that there is a hell. The elite are the minority and the masses are the majority. The elite are afraid of the masses finding out the secret that no one goes to hell. This is used to bridle (control) the masses. The elite fear that the masses will commit more sins. A good illustration of this is that if humanity knew when the world was going to end they would take it upon them-selves to destroy the earth including them-selves. The attempt can be made in several ways by eating, drinking, or smoking. Due to the mob mentality, they would be destroying property and massive riots would break out all over the world. The people in the world would lose their natural minds. I will reiterate; truth is not for the masses. Why? Due to the fact that all of us cannot handle the truth, some will not be able to comprehend it and others will not believe it. There are many people who came to America thinking that the streets were paved in gold. There are people who believe that the streets of heaven are paved in gold, suppose they're not. Can you handle it? What I am actually saying is these things do not have to exist in heaven for me. The presence of God is all that matters.

What we must believe there is only one God and He, Loves us all unconditionally. Put yourself in God's hands, the perfect hands that hold all things in place perfectly.

Time is a thief and a robber

Matthew: 26:18 (KJV) "And he said, Go into the city to such a man, and say unto him, The Master saith, My time is at hand; I will keep the pass-over at thy house with my disciples." The Merriam Webster Dictionary defines time as "a period during which an action, process, or condition exists or continues; a moment, hour, day, or year as indicated by a clock or calendar; a system reckoning time; a person's experience during a particular period (had a good *time*); the hours or days of one's work, an hourly pay rate (straight); time out."

Time is a thief and a robber

Christ dwelled here on earth for a period of time and gave his life for our salvation. Adam had no idea about time, but it became a factor after his fall. God revealed time to Adam and it's parallel to a world concept because time is a curse. It is twenty-four hours broken into twelve daytime hours and twelve nighttime hours. There is no day, night, or time in heaven. What exists is a continuous flow of God's unconditional Love.

There was another curse attached to time, man working by the sweat of his brow to earn a living. Today this does not apply only to men, women are also working by the sweat of their brow to earn a living.

At the time of Christ, people worked in the fields to earn a living. The workday began at the break of dawn in order to have as many daylight hours as possible for the daily duties. During the early evening it was the perfect time for Christ to preach the gospel to the people. The people were supposed to let a transformation take place within them individually. Time is a thief and a robber it has stolen from some of us on more than one occasion.

When you meet a person who has all the qualities you are looking for in a mate, he or she is either already married or too young to marry.

The thoughts that runs through your mind "Is time has cheated me." What time does is act like it has a mind of its own and just keeps on moving with or without you. What time reveals to you is that it is not your friend or lover. It is like a shadow, here and gone. You have no effect on time at all and it is not affected if you waste it. It can have an effect on us in different ways early in life. Some people skin wrinkles, others go gray or lose their hair. The way the world is designed, we need as much time as possible. You have heard of the expressions: "A woman's work is never done" and "Rome was not built in a day." There are not enough hours in the day so these expressions are true in many cases.

Certain things can only happen here in this world. What we need to realize is heaven has another answer and it's not a thief or a robber.

In the Book of Joshua: 10:12-13 tells us that the Lord delivered up the Amorites to the children of Israel. Joshua said in the sight of Israel, Sun, stand still upon Gibeon, and the Moon in the valley of Ajalon! The sun stood still and the moon stayed until the children of Israel were victorious over their enemies. The sun did not go down for a whole day. The omnipotence of God was shown when he suspended time for the children of Israel. Time is a thief and a robber.

We don't know how Christ is going to reveal himself to us or the time. Although we are living in a time of modern technology, it definitely cannot apprehend God or time. Don't think of our time on earth as being a long time, it's better to parallel our lives with God's sight. It can be finished on this side of the Jordan River within the blink of an eye.

Rising above the World

Mark: 4:19 (AMP) "Then the cares and anxieties of the world and distractions of the age, and the pleasure and delight and false glamour and deceitfulness of riches, and the craving and passionate desire for other things creep in and choke and suffocate the Word, and it becomes fruitless."

Mark: 8:36 (AMP) "For what does it profit a man to gain the whole world, and forfeit his life [in the eternal kingdom of God]?"

John: 8:23 (AMP) "And he said to them, you are from below; I am from above. You are of this world (of this earthly order); I am not of this world."

Rising above the World

I want to briefly discuss the importance of chastity and refer to the women and men who are still virgins. Do not allow yourself to be swayed by others coaching you to lose your virginity before marriage. There are so many people losing their virginity before marriage and that doesn't make it right. The people who are coaching you more than likely lost their virginity before marriage and misery loves company. Christ was a clear example that a holy life is not impossible to live on earth. He explained it through the parables as well. Christ was the answer right in front of the multitude.

However simplicity does not matter; some people refuse to or are unable to adapt. We are not expected to be robots or zombies, only obedient to God. Do not let the world desires choke or suffocate the word of God that is in you. God is eternal and we must seek him; the world will eventually pass away. The Bible tells us what happened to the first Adam in the garden and what happened to the second Adam on the cross. Although these two significant events occurred generations apart, they are still linked. They also link us together in this dimension. The world system is designed to freight you, your love ones and friends as a form of control. The perfect text to refer to is Psalm 23. Do not allow the world to be your God. Enoch and No'ah were examples of rising above the world and hell. It's sad to see humanities behavior is fulfilling predictions in the Bible daily and grieving God's heart. When you rise above the world, the most important element is to rise above temptation(s). The world is filled with them and the results can be critical or fatal for you and others. The world and temptation(s) go hand in hand and we continue to give them power over our lives. The world keeps us hypnotized by temptation(s) appearing to be so sweet, but in actuality is bitter like lemons. The temptation(s) are usually parallel to a person's weakness. When we look at the world from generation to generation, the people have been tempted by the least of things and continue to fall deeper and deeper. The world has caused us to be divided with an egotistical mind operating through nationalities, gender, or status. God is expecting us to rise to the level of not being strangers to him. Christ said: "The poor will always be with you," and he was absolutely right. There are people who are poor on so many levels—faith, happiness, health, and wealth. A good example: If the government gave every family on the planet a million dollars (there may be a few exceptions) but overall the people who were poor would still be poor. There are people who don't have a conscious for money.

It takes more time to obtain the money than for it to be spent. As for the rich people it goes without saying. It is well known that people are lovers of money and not God.

John: (AMP) 18:36 "Jesus answered, My kingdom (kinship, royal power) belongs not to this world. If My kingdom were of this world, My followers would have been fighting to keep Me from being handed over to the Jews. But as it is, My kingdom is not from here (this world); [it has no such origin or source]." There is a song with the following lyrics, "I want to run through the halls of my High School / I want to scream at the top of my lungs / I just found out there's NO SUCH THING as the real world / Just a lie you've got to rise above / I am invincible / I am invincible / I am invincible / As long as I'm alive." Humanities continuous foolish behavior reveals the failure to realize the world is not real.

This is sad but true: It revealed that humanity has fallen for the "OAKEY" DOKE", "BIG TIME". The world is an unconscious dimension of belief.

You are here on earth, but in reality, you are in Heaven.

God is in you and you are in him. Rising above the world is your spiritual food; seek God daily.

Still the Mercy of God

Genesis: 6:5-9 (KJV) "And GOD saw that the wickedness of man was great in the earth, and that every imagination of the thoughts of his heart was only evil continually.

6 And it repented the Lord that he had made man on earth, and it grieved him at his heart.

7 And the Lord said, I will destroy man whom I created from the face of the earth; both man, and the beast, and creeping thing, and the fowls of the air; for it repenteth me that I have made them.

8 But No'ah found favor in the eyes of the Lord.

9 These are the generations of No'ah: No'ah was a just man and perfect in his generations, and No'ah walked with God."

Genesis: 19:15-18 (KJV) "And when the morning arose, then the angels hastened Lot, saying, Arise, take thy wife, and thy two daughters, which are here; lest thou be consumed in the iniquity of the city.

16 And while he lingered, the men laid hold upon his hand, and upon the hand of his wife, and upon the hand of his two daughters; the LORD being merciful unto him: and they brought him forth, and set him without the city.

17 And it came to pass, when they had brought them forth abroad, that he said, Escape for thy life; look not behind thee neither stay thou in all the plain; escape to
the mountain, lest thou be consumed. 18
And Lot said unto them, Oh not so, my Lord:"

Genesis: 19:19-22 (KJV) "Behold now, thy servant hath found grace in thy sight, and thou hast magnified thy mercy, which thou hast shewed unto me in saving my life; and I cannot escape to the mountain, lest some evil take me, and I die:

20 Behold now, this city is near to flee unto, and it is a little one: Oh, let me escape thither, (is it not a little one?) and my soul shall live. 21 And he said unto him, See, I have accepted thee concerning this thing also, that I will not overthrow this city, for the which thou hast spoken.

22 Haste thee, escape thither; for I cannot do anything till thou be come thither. Therefore the name of the city was called Zo'ar."

Still the Mercy of God

God is patient and long-suffering. However we can see it clearly stated in the Bible that God has allowed judgment to come on the earth. He is a jealous God and has expressed in the Bible that humanity must not choose any other gods over him. The Ego's spirit operating through humanity has no reverential awe for God. In the generation of No'ah God sought the hearts of the people and found one man, No'ah. "No'ah was a just man and perfect; he found favor in God's eyes. No'ah was instructed by God to build the ark and bring two of every living thing, male and female, into the ark for procreation. However, the people were unable to conceive the significance of the ark, which kept them from changing from disobedient to obedient. The flood might not have happened. The people were allowed into the ark to escape the flood. They chose otherwise and brought on their own calamity in that generation. We have the power as well to cause our own trials and tribulations.

Christ going to the cross 2000 years ago instead of judging humanity showed Mercy and Grace, John: 5:30 reveals it. God has given humanity power over the four elements in this dimension: earth, air, fire and water. These elements must be used appropriately, if they are abused, instead of obtaining an action or positive results, you will have a reaction with negative results. The same thing applies to our lives concerning obedience or disobedience to God. There was another man God had mercy for, Lot. The angels led Lot and his family out of Sodom and Gomorrah and they arrived safely in a city called Zoar.

We must face facts and acknowledge that our conduct is detrimental to our well-being. No'ah and Lot showed themselves to be separate from others in their generation. They were God's chosen, sole survivors for humanity in the Old Testament.

These sole survivors in the Old Testament were leading up to the New Testament. Still the mercy of God, the ultimate Soul Savior for humanity Christ, King of Kings and Lord of Lords!

The 144,000 Chosen Ones

Revelation: 7:4 (KJV) "And I heard the number of them which were sealed: and there were sealed an hundred and forty and four thousand of all the tribes of the children of Israel."

This is referring to Revelation: 7:4.

1. Judah
2. Reuben
3. Gad
4. Aser
5. Nepthalim
6. Manasses
7. Simeon
8. Levi
9. Issachar
10. Zabulon

11. Joseph
12. Benjamin

These are the 144,000 from the tribes of Israel.

Revelation: 14:1, 3-5 (KJV)

The 144,000 Chosen Ones

"And I looked, and, lo a Lamb stood on the mount Sion and with him an hundred forty and four thousand, having his Father's name written in their foreheads. And they sung as it were a new song before the throne, and before the four beasts, and the elders: and no man could learn that song but the hundred and forty and four thousand, which were redeemed from the earth. These are they which were not defiled with women; for they are virgins. These are they which follow the Lamb whithersoever he goeth. These were redeemed from among men, being the first fruits unto God and to the Lamb. And in their mouth was found no guile: for they are without fault before the throne of God."

The Lamb, the Messiah, the Exalted and Anointed one

The name that is, above all names the Son Christ. The 144,000 with him are men, women, and children. The book of Genesis said that in the Garden of Eden, God created male and female. They were designed to bring balance into this realm.

The 144,000 each have a spiritual soul mate present. They are assigned to go out into the world two by two, parallel to the animals entering Noah's ark, and become one bright light in the universe. They are the light of the world.

The 144,000 chosen ones consist of 12,000 for each tribe and considered to be a house under the name. The tribes are residing within the communities and will come forth at the appropriate time. These 144,000 are chosen out of each nationality and the rainbow is a representation.

The 144,000 are universal beings as well as spiritual beings because Love is a universal language and universal in itself.

Mark: 13:20 (KJV) "And except that the Lord had shortened those days, no flesh should be saved: but for the elect's sake, whom he hath chosen, he hath shortened the days."

This parallel scripture refers to the twelve disciples who walked with Christ in that day and also the twelve tribes of Israel, the makeup of the 144,000 in this day. These chosen ones were predestined by God before they ever came into existence. The 144,000 were expected to relinquish their free will and surrender themselves to the will of God, He chose and anointed them.

The Father's name, written in their foreheads, is the Father's signature. The 144,000 are eternally sealed to him through his will. Their names are certainly written in the Lamb's Book of Life. There is a song that resides within the 144,000 throughout their entire being; it will be birthed through them. They will sing out praises throughout eternity from their true being: his spirit.

These will be in the presence of God and the entire heavenly host. It is the song of thanksgiving to God for redeeming them.

John: 17:15 (KJV) "I pray not that thou shouldest take them out of the world, but thou shouldest keep them from the evil."

These chosen ones are not taken home to glory in the invisible realm of the present perception. God's divine protection never leaves them, and they are not seduced by the evil one, the Ego.

1Thessalonians: 4:16 (KJV) "And the dead in Christ will rise first:"

In the Book of 1 Thessalonians: 4:17 tells us the remaining living ones and those resurrected from the dead will be caught up together in the clouds to meet the Lord in the air. The 144,000 chosen ones and the saints are not going anywhere this is the actual rapture that will take place. Heaven will be transformed right before their eyes a place like the Garden of Eden. The Spirit Realm is where nothing ungodly will be able to deceive anything in order to enter. They live in the spirit realm like God beings, the celestial body and the quickening of the spirit. They will experience heaven continuously and this is a reversal of what happened in the Garden of Eden. It is actually seeing through the eyes of Christ.

Matthew: 24:36 (KJV) "But of that [exact] day and hour no one knows, not even the angels of heaven, nor the Son, but only the Father."

Christ does not need to know the day or hour. He was God the Father that allowed the judgment to fall on the people in the Old Testament, and Christ with compassion in the New Testament. Christ will be God the Father with the judgment again for the spiritually lost in this generation. The judgment will take place in the presence of God the Eternal Light in heaven within the blink of an eye.

2 Corinthians: 5:10 (KJV) "For we all must appear before the judgment seat of Christ; that every one may receive the things done in his body, according to that he hath done, whether it be good or bad."

At the appointed time the saints will go before the judgment seat of Christ in heaven to be judged. Although we believe through faith that God will forgive by repenting now.

The judging will take place within the blink of an eye as well. Everyone will be judged according to their deed(s). Once the judging begins there is no turning back. In the meantime we need to seek God and inquire about our short comings before this inevitable event takes place. The 144,000 were only able to see the way God designed them in truth. The 144,000 are virgins in spirit they are pure in spirit, light, love heart and truth.

John: 10:27 "My sheep hear my voice, and I know them, and they follow me:" They are seeking God and nothing else; consciously and subconsciously their faith is in him. It is their heart's desire to fulfill his will.

When you look throughout the Bible, you will see that God chose people in every generation for his purpose. The 144,000 are a nation that will be revealed in this generation.

The saints are to honor the Lord by giving him the first fruits of their earnings, 10 percent. It is elementary the 10 percent blesses the other 90 percent. The 144,000 chosen ones are God's first fruits, his 10 percent out of humanity souls. They will add blessings to the rest of humanity through their ministry.

Matthew: 24:14 (KJV) "And this gospel of the kingdom shall be preached in all the

world for a witness unto all nations; and then shall the end come."
Let us look at this, mathematically, 72 degrees times 5 degrees equals 360 degrees, a full circle. The 144,000 will cover this entire realm with the word of God.

Luke: 4:18-19 (KJV) "THE SPIRIT OF THE LORD IS UPON ME, BECAUSE HE HATH ANOINTED ME TO PREACH THE GOSPEL TO THE POOR; HE HATH SENT ME TO HEAL THE BROKERNHEARTED, TO PREACH DELIVERANCE TO THE CAPTIVES, AND RECOVERING OF SIGHT TO THE BLIND, TO SET AT LIBERTY THEM THAT ARE BRUISED,
19 TO PREACH THE ACCEPTANCE YEAR OF THE LORD".

We speak of the second coming of Christ. This is the second coming of Christ's Ministry.
These scriptures are imperative to me, because it is the ending of world time and thinking the return back to Eternity.

Do you really know when God appears?

Matthew: 25:1-13 (KJV) THEN SHALL the kingdom of heaven be likened unto ten virgins, which took their lamps, and went forth to meet the bridegroom. And five of them were wise, and five were foolish. They that were foolish took their lamps, and took no oil with them: But the wise took oil in their vessels with their lamps. While the bridegroom tarried, they all slumbered and slept. And at midnight there was a cry made, Behold, the bridegroom cometh; go ye out to meet him. Then all those virgins arose, and trimmed their lamps. And the foolish said unto the wise, Give us of your oil; for our lamps are gone out. But the wise answered, saying, Not so; lest there be not enough for us and you: but go ye rather to them that sell, and buy for yourselves. And while they went to buy, the bridegroom came; and they that were ready went in with him to the marriage: and the door was shut. Afterward came also the other virgins, saying, Lord, Lord, open to us. But he answered and said, Verily, I say unto you, I know you not. Watch therefore, for ye know neither the day nor hour wherein the Son of man cometh."

Do you really know when God appears?

When celebrities have children, their births are heard all around the world. The birth of Christ did not have a big celebration. It was a pre-shift that took place in the earth. There were only a few who understood the significance: Simone, the three wise men, King Herod, the Chief-Priests, and the Scribes. Some people thought that John the Baptist was Christ. Although John never professed that he was Christ, he spoke of his coming. We must be careful; the first one is usually the counterfeit. This was an ultimate test of the spirit. Christ came in his Father's name and was not received.

The people were unaware of whom or what was their foundation. This explains Matthew:24:24 (KJV) "For there shall arise false Christ's, and false prophets, and shall shew great signs and wonders; insomuch that, if it were possible, they shall deceive the very elect."

Revelation: 3:3 (KJV) "I will come on thee as a thief, and thou shall not know what hour I will come upon thee." Our relationship with Christ is not the same, but there are others that don't have a relationship with him. The appearance of God can have an impact on us in several ways. A Revelation an Epiphany, a Shift, or the Day of Atonement.

The five wise virgins had on the whole armor of God, but the five foolish virgins did not. Do not let people shake your foundation. Hebrews: 12:1 (KJV) "Wherefore seeing we also are compassed about with so great a cloud of witnesses, let us lay aside every weight, and the sin which doth so easily beset us, and let us run with patience the race that is set before us," The church is looking for Christ to return floating on a cloud and expecting to meet him in the air. It is not that Christ will come on a cloud and we meet him in the air, but rather we connect with him through faith. There will be a crowd of people around Christ trying to touch him, like the woman with the issue of blood. At this time, you will be able to see him physically. Do not think its impossible; I had my vision of Christ some years ago. The spirit and light of God was in flesh.

What gave me confirmation that it was Christ, I was in the right position, on my knees in a partial prostrate position at His Feet. He allowed me to continue to look at him. Christ's beautiful black eyes were looking through me and holding nothing against me. Peace rested within his entire being. Christ never blinked; he showed me a big, round light like the sun and spoke to me telepathically. He said, "This is God." When I blinked, the vision of Christ was gone. There is a song with the following lyrics, "Do you know this man of Galilee / come to set the captive free? / Yes, I know the Man". I have met the man Christ! Some of us are experiencing the presence of God through angels disguised as ordinary people. When we look in the New Testament, it revealed how the disciples behaved in Christ's presence so many times.

Christ continued to perform miracles to assist them in becoming and remaining aware of him. The five foolish virgins were at the first Adam's level after his fall. The five wise virgins were at the second Adam's level. Although there is a waiting period for Christ to reveal himself, our lifetime here is actually like a night-watch service always expecting him.

There are so many people today who behave like the disciples or the five foolish virgins. What Christ said has been confirmed and what Christ did has been confirmed. The question you need to ask yourself is, "Will I be ready when Christ reveals himself?" The shift that takes place is in the mind: go with the flow or miss the flow but it is all up to you.

Do not allow your inner being to be like a waterfall and the key word here is *fall*!

I will ask you the imperative question again. Do you really know when God appears? It is the Eternal One within that is able to keep you from falling revealed.

One Breath, One Blood

Ecclesiastes: 3:19 (KJV) "For that which befalleth the sons of men befalleth beasts; even one thing befalleth them: as the one dieth, so dieth the other; yea they have all one breath; so that a man hath no preeminence above a beast: for all is vanity."
Ecclesiastes: 3:19 (AMP) "For that which befalls the sons of men befalls beasts: even [in the end] one thing befalls them both. As the one dies, so dies the other. Yes, they all have one breath and spirit, so that a man has no preeminence over a beast; for all is vanity (emptiness, falsity, and futility)"!

Acts: 17:26 (KJV) "And hath made of one blood all nations of men for to dwell on all the face of the earth, and hath determined the times before appointed, and the bounds of their habitation."

Acts: 17:26 (AMP) "And He made from one [common origin, one source, one blood] all nations of men to settle on the face of the earth, having definitely determined [their] allotted periods of time and the fixed boundaries of their habitation (their settlements, lands and abodes)."

One Breath, One Blood

Our lives are one breath and one blood in this dimension. The breath and blood are life in a second-to-second cycle. We don't know where the next breath can be taken; it is that simple. The lack of oxygen and the excessive loss of blood can kill a person. The breath and blood are designed in this dimension to flow throughout the human body. The breath and blood are in alignment. We take breathing for granted until it becomes difficult to do and the blood needs oxygen to survive. The Bible tells us that God breathed one breath into the first Adam and he became a living soul.

The soul awakened and caused the breath and blood to flow for the body to function according to God's will. The one breath and one blood they're essential. It began with one breath—in other words the invisible spirit. We can see that the journey in this dimension can easily be ended through illness, murder, suicide, or natural causes ect.

Although the breath or blood can be attacked, God is still in the healing business.

He is an eternal healing being. The one breath and one blood are experienced from a world perspective and connect us all together. We are donators to each other in order to save lives. One of Christ's parables says that if a man has one hundred sheep and one has gone astray, he will leave the other ninety-nine and seek the one who has gone astray. When the sheep is found, there is rejoicing. Although Christ was referring to humanity the one breath and one blood is also in animals. We must rise to the level that hatred no longer exist in the world man versus man, man versus beast or beast versus beast. God gave animals a spirit, soul, and body. This is why animals of every kind had to be included on "Noah's" ark. Ecclesiastes: 3:19 and Acts:17:26 these two scriptures are vital to understanding creation.

God loved us first by breathing his breath into man and beast and simultaneously supplying blood to run through our veins.

The one breath and one blood of God and our body made us living beings. The combined Spirit and Light of God that dwells within made us God Beings.

God's Creation

Isaiah: 45:7 (KJV) "I form the light, and create darkness: I make peace, and create evil: I the Lord do all these things".

Revelation: 3:16 (KJV) "So then because thou art lukewarm, and neither cold nor hot, I will spue thee out of my mouth."

God's Creation

There are two significant dimensions within humanities being. One is the dimension of eternal light and the other is the dimension of darkness. God has given humanity the opportunity to choose one of these dimensions light (heaven) or darkness (the world). The Eternal Light and Darkness dwell within the heart of man as well as the Word of God. The waging of war between the eternal light and darkness occurs here. An old expression "There is a little bit of bad in every good little girl." These two dimensions are actually two characteristics. The characteristic of darkness is revealed more than the characteristic of light. We need to look at the key words here: One is *light* meaning good and the other is *dark*, meaning bad. The light dimension is aware of God and everything else, doubt does not exist. The dark dimension is unaware to an extent.

In the Book of Genesis: 6:5-7 talks about the wickedness of man and their thoughts being acted out. Humanity did whatever, wherever, whenever and however without being aware of God.

There are people who choose to have an idle mind and idle, hands they go hand and hand. Christ not only gave us salvation and eternal life but peace as well, peace beyond all human understanding. Christ's words of greeting to the disciples (after his resurrection when the disciples were in the room together behind closed doors in fear of the Jews were) "Peace, be unto you" (John 20:19).

Christ's departing words to the woman who washed his feet with her tears and wiped them with her hair. She anointed his feet with ointment. He said to the woman, "Thy faith hath saved thee: go in peace" (Luke 7:50).

I will reiterate God has given humanity the opportunity to choose one of these dimensions light (heaven) or darkness (the world).

God's attribute of omnipotence formed the light and created darkness. We know that all of humanity is in the image of God.

Let us examine this a little further; darkness exists in the things created and they're limited. The things he formed are light and not limited. Jeremiah: 1:5 reveals it. Humanity is also the Light of God, not a creation but a formation of a nation. God is the Eternal Light that dwells in everyone. We must maintain a level that does not require believing in a "devil" or "hell" to keep us obedient to God. I don't need a "devil" or "hell" as a scare tactic to keep me obedient, God is enough! Do not give the dimension of darkness the comfort of having faith in it. The sad part is people have fallen so deep into the belief of darkness. This will cause them to continue to sin. Everyone on the planet, dimension of darkness collectively will cause the devilish behavior and a hellacious dimension. The dimension of eternal light and the dimension of darkness cannot be balanced because one has all power and the other does not really exist. In the Book of Genesis: 16:2-6, we see that Sarai had her own idea. Do you think that God told Sarai to tell Abram to be intimate with Hagar? Absolutely Not! When you have a situation with three people, whether it is two women and one man or two men and one woman, this is a triangle which creates confusion. We have the one breath of God and two dimensions, one of eternal light and the other of darkness, within us, and it is like a triangle. When the dimension of darkness is removed, instead of a triangle, a straight line transforms. The one breath of God and the dimension of Eternal Light the straight and narrow road, it is the only road seen at that level. It is a road designed for living a Holy Spirit—Filled Life, a Sigh of Eternal Relief Peace.

God's Divine Protection

Exodus: 23:20 (KJV) "Behold, I send an Angel before thee, to keep thee in the way, and to bring thee into the place which I prepared". John: 16:7 (KJV) "Nevertheless I tell you the truth; It is expedient for you that I go away: for if I go not away, the Comforter will not come unto you; but if I depart, I will send him unto you."

God's Divine Protection

We are continuously protected by the Holy Spirit God's divine protection. Ephesians: 4:30 "And grieve not the Holy Spirit of God, whereby ye are sealed unto the day of redemption." In the Book of 1 Thessalonians: 5:19 is also referring to the Holy Spirit. Humanity should not insult, blaspheme, grieve, lie to, resist, or quench the Holy Spirit. The Holy Spirit is actually the Wife of God. This is why God instructs us not to do anything against the Holy Spirit. The first Adam was designed to respect Eve's femininity, because God respects the Holy Spirit's femininity.

In the Book of Acts: 2:1, the believers were on one accord in faith, not just in one place.

The people were filled with the Holy Ghost and they spoke in different tongues. The Holy Spirit's spiritual gifts can operate through us at the same level they operated in Christ's ministry. However the spiritual gifts can be used for a person's greed. It is like making Christ obsolete and sneaking past him to get to the Father or the Mother the Holy Spirit. Christ is the universal key to entering the kingdom. A person must first accept Christ as his or her Lord and Savior. Once Christ is accepted the person can freely move about throughout the kingdom. This will not only allow the person to pray to Christ the Son, but to the Father or the Mother the Holy Spirit. It does not matter which person you pray to in the trinity; all three persons hear the prayer. They will be in agreement with the answer you receive. God's heart does not rule his head, and it is impossible for him to make a mistake. God knew the anointing as well as the appropriate spiritual gift(s) to coincide with our spirit. The spiritual gift(s) are designed for a life time. The Eternal Family has designed the family on earth as a traditional family a father, a mother and children that reveals, so as is above, so as is below. Our Eternal Father blessed us with a physical mother here on earth. She was put here to nurture, to teach us morals and values.

We are also blessed with an Eternal Mother.

However society has failed to reveal, that the Holy Spirit is our Eternal Mother, God's divine protection. There are times when our physical mother abandons us but our eternal mother never has and never will abandon us. I will reiterate: do not insult, blaspheme, grieve, lie to, resist, or quench the Holy Spirit. There is a price to pay with your soul for such acts. The Holy Spirit will be the witness.

It is not by God's might or by his power but by his Spirit, our Eternal Mother the Holy Spirit.

The First Adam / The Fall of Man

Genesis: 1:27 (KJV) "So God created man in his own image, in the image of God created he him; male and female created he them." The word *image* in the Merriam Webster Dictionary defines it as "optical of a thing as produced by a reflection in a mirror or through a lens." Before the fall of man took place God enjoyed watching himself, running around in the garden playing. The spirit can be fleshed and clothed.

Genesis: 1:28 (KJV) "And God blessed them, and God said unto them, Be fruitful, and multiply, and replenish the earth, and subdue it: and have dominion over the fish of the sea, and over the fowl of the air, and over every living thing that moveth upon the earth." After the fall of man, life became complicated. Genesis: 2:15 (AMP) "And the Lord God took the man and put him in the Garden of Eden to tend and guard and keep it." This was the first commandment, God had instructed Adam to tend and guard the garden. He failed to detect the serpent, with an ungodly spirit had entered the garden. Adam was unaware that breaking the first commandment had initially allowed him to be set up to fall. What actually happened in the Garden of Eden Adam was directly told by the Lord God. This was before Adam and Eve became individual God beings they shared the same body. The womb was initially carried by Adam. Eve was taken out of Adam and when Eve became a God being, the womb was transferred to her. Eve is called "woman" because she was taken out of man and also carries the womb.

Genesis: 2:16-17 (KJV) "And the Lord God commanded the man, saying, Of every tree of the garden thou mayest freely eat: But of the tree of the knowledge of good and evil, thou shalt not eat of it: for in the day that thou eatest thereof thou shalt surely die." This was the second commandment God placed on man, Adam not Eve. 1 Corinthians: 11:3 (KJV) "But I would have you know, that the head of every man is Christ; and the head of the woman is the man; and the head of Christ is God." Adam and Eve were God in flesh and enthroned to rule the Garden of Eden equally it is a kingdom. They were one with their dimension in heaven God beings. In the Book of Genesis: 3:2-5 tells us how the serpent, sought out the woman, the tender part of man.

Genesis: 3:6 (KJV) "And when the woman saw that the tree was good for food, and that it was pleasant to the eyes, and a tree to be desired to make one wise, she took of the fruit thereof, and did eat, and gave also unto her husband with her; and he did eat." Eve ate from the tree of the knowledge of good and evil. Eve could have eaten from the tree all day long and nothing would have happened. Eve's conscious remained in the heaven realm. There is no record indicating when Eve came to Adam and he took what was forbidden. It was Adam's continuous obedience to God's second commandment that kept them from becoming spiritually lost. Then Adam took of what was forbidden.

This is when they both became spiritually lost.

When a person's focus is in the wrong place, he or she has a tendency to use poor judgment.

Let us look at this a little more closely.

Adam's fall from grace prevented him from dwelling in the spirit realm heaven.

Isaiah: 45:7 (KJV) "I form the light, and create darkness: I make peace, and create evil: I the LORD do all these things".

This revealed the transformation that took place within Adam.

Adam no longer focused on God's will; he developed an "Ego".

The spirit realm became unknown to him and free will began in the mind of humanity. Our thoughts and actions are free will and are not always in alignment with God's will. We must be careful with free will because it's a form of being spiritually lost or disobedient and it causes us to continuously break God's commandments. Adam bowed his head and kneeled to the Ego and relinquished his throne to ungodliness.

This was taken as a form of worshipping in a mundane dimension, not the spirit realm. They were disconnected from their true being, God. Due to eating from the tree of the knowledge of (good and evil), their eyes were blinded from the truth and things became obscured.

When we look at Paul in the New Testament, it is revealed that the opposite happened to him. He could only see God's way, the truth. Adam and Eve could not see God's way. They were no longer God beings; they had become human beings. Their bodies transformed from the tree of eternal life (celestial heaven bodies), to the tree of the knowledge of good and evil (terrestrial earth bodies). This body, the tree of the knowledge of good and evil, is parallel to the knowledge of sin sickness and death. Adam and Eve became flesh conscious, focusing only on the flesh. Both entities were tainted and the two of them completed one another. They became one with a mundane dimension lower than themselves. They begin to believe in things that were contradictory to God: lack, sickness, and death. The phase "Believe it and you will receive it", whether consciously, subconsciously or unconsciously, somehow, you make it real to yourself.

Genesis: 3:9 (KJV) "And the Lord God called unto Adam and said unto him, Where art thou?" God was not saying to Adam, "Where are you? I cannot find you." One of God's attribute's omniscience God was saying, "You have disconnected from me your true being." Adam disconnected from God and took on a world perspective of life. The heavens were no longer seen or experienced continuously.

God so lovingly blessed Adam with the keys to the kingdom. This is the eternal one giving Adam not just dominion over everything he created but eternal power. The word *dominion* in the Merriam Webster Dictionary defines it as "supreme authority". God is the only, Supreme Being who has eternal power, so he is the only one who can give it. The same thing applies to us today, the eternal power of God is within us and He's waiting to operate through us. Adam was given eternal power over everything God created except for the tree of the knowledge of good and evil. Let us review this in its essence.

There are two imperative questions that has haunted humanity:

> Was it a real tree? God was the tree of the knowledge of good and evil because He was the only one who had knowledge of good and evil. God is within us and all around us. God is also eternal life, a spirit, and he breathed himself into man.
> Was it a real piece of fruit? 1 Corinthians: 2:16 (KJV) "FOR WHO HATH KNOWN THE MIND OF THE LORD, THAT HE MAY INSTRUCT HIM? But we have the mind of Christ." It was the God conscious. The God conscious and the mind of Christ are one. The first Adam was blessed with God's conscious. Adam did not have dominion over

God's conscious God and his conscious are one.

Let us look further into the unveiling of God's word. Genesis: 3:22 (KJV) "And the Lord God said, Behold, the man is become as one of us, to know good and evil: and now, lest he put forth his hand, and take also of the tree of life, and eat, and live forever:" Adam instantly transformed into a lost soul when he approached God without a humble heart. He was attempting to be God, over God the Supreme Being and would have remained spiritually lost forever. There was no way man could reconnect with God and become spiritually awakened again this is the ego's fate. I will reiterate: God made your body, the tree of eternal life, his dwelling place. God is within us and all around us and we have absolutely no dominion over God.

Genesis: 3:23 (KJV) "Therefore the Lord God sent him forth from the Garden of Eden, to till the ground from whence he was taken." When God sent the man forth from the Garden, it was mercy and grace combined for humanity. Adam was unable to fully reconnect with God since he had a world perspective on life.

I want to refer back to the serpent or the Ego's, deceit for Adam. The serpent (Ego) was trying to get the God conscious from man and was unsuccessful, it was only able to cause man to fall out of the God conscious through the woman.

Matthew: 4:1 (KJV) "Then was Jesus led up of the Spirit into the wilderness to be tempted of the devil." This was a test to see if Jesus being in flesh would slide, slip, or miss the mark. It is actually the Ego's free will that causes one to fall short of the glory of God. If Jesus had allowed the Ego to take control of his being, he would have missed his destiny of going to the cross. I will reiterate: our thoughts and actions are free will and not always in alignment with God's will. We must be careful it is a form of being spiritually lost.

The Ego has been surviving off of our free will, or our disobedience. The Ego made an attempt in the New Testament to make it self real to Christ in the wilderness.

Matthew: 4:7 (KJV) "Jesus said unto him, It is written again, THOU SHALT NOT TEMPT THE LORD THY GOD." The Ego was still unsuccessful; Christ did not fall in his conscious, even in the flesh. Christ is part of the God-Head. The Ego thought if it could obtain God's conscious. God's Glory, Omnipresence, Omniscience, Omnipotence, Immutability and Eternity would all belong to it, but God and his attributes are one.

Job: 1:1 (KJV) "There was a man in the land of Uz, whose name was Job; and one that was perfect and upright and feared God and eschewed evil."

Job not only had patience, but also the God conscious and dwelled in heaven. This is why Job was blessed prior to his test and abundantly thereafter focusing only on God. Once the God conscious operates through you continuously, you have overcome the world and dwell in heaven.

Lovemaking

Genesis: 1:27 (KJV) "So God created man in his own image, in the image of God created he him; male and female created he them." 1 Corinthians: 13:1-13 explained that all we need is love, because without it, we are nothing.

God not only created us in the image of himself, he also allowed one of the ultimate pleasures in this dimension beside himself: lovemaking. Some of us have been blessed with a soul mate. This person may come once in a lifetime or came in past lives. There are others who were not ordained to have a soul mate. God is able to keep you chaste and has not put the desire in your heart for a mate. We all have a conscious and the person that you marry shares the qualities of your conscious. At a wedding, the union of a man and a woman take place; it is a priceless act showing how much you love each other.

1 Corinthians: 7:4 (KJV) "The wife hath not power of her own body, but the husband: and likewise also the husband hath not power of his own body, but the wife." I want to make this perfectly clear: although a husband or a wife does not have power over his or her own body, it is imperative that the lovemaking be consensual.

God does not force himself on anyone and knowing when to engage in lovemaking or not is imperative. It is not the right time if you or your spouse, are physically ill, depressed, or intoxicated. The two of you will not be able to reciprocate the ultimate energy during lovemaking it will be defiled. God who dwells within the two of you is not being expressed. The intimacy between a husband and wife is so sacred, the heavenly host is supposed to be the only witness. 1 Corinthians: 2:16 (KJV) "FOR WHO HATH KNOWN THE MIND OF THE LORD, THAT HE MAY INSTRUCT

HIM? But we have the mind of Christ." You are supposed to make love to one another's mind. The lovemaking should not be rushed into, tearing off each other's clothes like animals. It does not give you a license to act like a freak; remember, we are made in the image of God! The husband and wife's approach toward one another has to demonstrate respect of the highest. The husband and wife are opening their entire beings as well as their hearts. The energy of God within them flows back and forth from one another, feeding each other's spirit and soul. Let us not forget the temple of God, the body, is also being fed from the crown of the head to the soles of the feet. When you are sleeping, your spirit travels to other dimensions and allows you to dream. The spirit is supposed to travel during lovemaking as well. When the husband's spirit and the wife's spirit are clear, it brings balance.

2 Peter: 3:8 (KJV) "But, beloved, be not ignorant of this one thing, that one day is with the Lord as a thousand years, and a thousand years as one day."

You are entering dimensions that are ultimately pleasurable, and if you had your way, you would not come back. It is an ultimate state of conscious eternal comfort. Have you ever eaten a piece of candy that was sweet and sour and got your juices flowing? Lovemaking is a pleasurable pain because every movement is not the same. When you experience the Holy Ghost, you either laugh or cry. This is for the men: It is okay to cry during lovemaking; you will not be emasculated, let it out. The tears are only stars it's your time to shine. The two of you are at the mercy seat and the humbleness prevents one from overpowering the other. We have seen demonstrations of people put under hypnosis.

The person focuses only on the object that is waved back and forth in front of his or her eyes.

There are people who will try to or have hypnotized other people under the spell of their male or female genital. The Trinity does not overpower each other and they're always in agreement it is balance. During lovemaking, the husband's and wife's bodies meet perfectly with masculinity and femininity entwining together to become one. When this takes place male and female no longer exist.

This is the angelic spirit soaring through the universe like an eagle. What makes it more exciting and inviting every time the husband and wife make love is it supposed to be adventurous and mind-blowing. This is God taking full control of the two of you and you're going through the realms of heaven in ecstasy. When certain movements are made during lovemaking, you are able to know if he or she will give you a verbal response. It is wonderful to talk to each other during lovemaking, but not in a dirty way. I will reiterate: we are made in the image of God! If the husband and wife are unable to reach a state of ecstasy during lovemaking, there may be an imbalance in the chemistry. Your spouse or you may no longer be able to tap into the other's treasures during lovemaking. The husband and wife have to be familiar with each other's emotions during lovemaking. If your spouse is performing in a way which indicates he or she is not in the same dimension with you, you should stop making love immediately there are two possible reasons. One is infidelity may have been committed by one of you, the other is that he or she is imaging making love to someone else and focused on that person; only their body is with you. He or she may call out that person's name, and this can be devastating to you. We must understand the severity of going outside of the marriage and having sex. Because when you have sex with person (s) other than your spouse, all of the other people that person had sex with are having sex with you. You bring the energy to your spouse and this becomes an open door for whatever or whoever energy to invade your relationship. It is like giving your spouse a transmittable disease. What makes it different is it's an invisible spirit and exchanged through the energy. This may be a one-night stand for you. The energy may not have too much of an effect on you but you can become a carrier and your spouse may become bound by it. Sometimes it can cause a person to become promiscuous and he or she loses their identity through an unconscious state. An inability to rise above the negative energy develops. I don't want to sound too harsh, but the couple may be starting a family. When an unborn child is coming through the matrix, the birth canal, the negative energy can attach itself to him or her. The negative energy was introduced through a sexual act.

The child can enter the world with physical or psychological problems, or God forbid, die. Your behavior brought it onto an innocent child.

I will reiterate: this is why the husband's spirit and the wife's spirit have to be clear. God entrusted the first Adam with the Garden of Eden, and he defiled himself. Since that time humanity has continuously defiled themselves through their unconscionable sexual activities and the misuse of other creations. The Trinity, the three persons of God the, I AM, the one and only dwelling universal Love, does not want lovemaking to be overrated or understated, only perfect.

This sermon has expressed that you need the seventh gift of the Holy Spirit, the spiritual gift of discernment of spirits. We all need this gift to operate through us every second of the day.

The Resurrected Life

We have been here several lifetimes. The resurrected life can exist without departing from this dimension. The resurrection has been waiting on us to be resurrected Christ. God made the resurrected life simple for us. The answer dwells within us and in the written word.

Matthew: 22:37-40 (KJV) "Jesus said unto him, THOU SHALT LOVE THE LORD THY GOD WITH ALL THY HEART, AND WITH ALL THY SOUL, AND WITH ALL THY MIND. This is the first great commandment. And the second is like unto it, THOU SHALT LOVE THY NEIGHBOUR AS THYSELF. On these two commandments hang all the law and the prophets."

The two commandments bind together and become one.

Once the fall of man—the first Adam—took place, this commandment became our test here on earth.

About the Book

Heaven is speaking to us from all aspects of life. The millennium has induced an urge in people to seek the hidden answers and catapulted us into the quest for life. There is no more revolving-door syndrome; you are exiting the comfort zone and entering new possibilities. The book is composed of short scripture revelations and sermons. This is heaven's way of revealing the simplicity of obtaining the hidden answers.

The question heaven is asking is: "Are you a seeker?" If yes, then seek and you shall find. The quest in life is revealed in 1 Corinthians: 15:53. "For this corruptible must put on incorruption, and this mortal must put on immortality."

www.ingramcontent.com/pod-product-compliance
Ingram Content Group UK Ltd.
Pitfield, Milton Keynes, MK11 3LW, UK
UKHW041943190726
13854UKWH00004B/1759

9 781452 090672